Little Red R[i...]

The Cha[...]

 Narrator

 Mother

 Red Riding Hood

 Wolf

 Gran

 Woodcutter

This book is dedicated to William Krueger

Narrator: Once upon a time, there was a girl named Little Red Riding Hood.

 Mother: I want you to take these hot pancakes to Gran.

 Narrator: So Little Red Riding Hood went off into the woods.

Narrator: On the way, a wolf smelled the pancakes. He ran to Gran's house.

 Wolf: Knock, knock.

 Gran: Who's there?

 Wolf: Boo!

 Gran: Boo who?

 Wolf: Don't cry. It's just me

4

Narrator: The wolf ran inside. He locked Gran in the cupboard and he put on her hat and glasses. Then he climbed into her bed.

Red Riding Hood: I've brought you some pancakes for lunch, Gran.

Wolf: I've got a bit of a sore throat today.

 Red Riding Hood: You do sound a bit funny. And, Gran, what big ears you have!

 Wolf: All the better to hear you with, my dear!

Red Riding Hood:
And, Gran, what
big eyes you have!

 Wolf: All the better
to see you with, my dear!

 Red Riding Hood:
And, Gran, what
a big nose you have!

 Wolf: All the better
to smell you with, my dear!

Red Riding Hood:
And, Gran, what
big teeth you have!

Wolf: All the better
to eat the pancakes with,
my dear!

Narrator: And he reached
for the pancakes. He was
just about to gobble them
up when there was a knock
at the door.

12

Narrator: In came the woodcutter.

 Woodcutter: Wally, I have told you before, you are not to eat other people's lunches! You are grounded for a week!

 Narrator: The woodcutter let Gran out of the cupboard and took his pet wolf home.

Red Riding Hood: Gran, let's go out for lunch today!